SMALL BATHROOMS
PETITES SALLES DE BAINS
KLEINE BADEZIMMER

cirencester
college
a beacon college

SMALL BATHROOMS
PETITES SALLES DE BAINS
KLEINE BADEZIMMER

evergreen

EVERGREEN is an imprint of

Taschen GmbH

© 2005 TASCHEN GmbH

Hohenzollernring 53, D-50672 Köln

www.taschen.com

Editor Editrice Redakteur:
Simone Schleifer

French translation Traduction française Französische Übersetzung:
Marion Westerhoff

English translation Traduction anglaise Englische Übersetzung:
Nadja Leonard

Proof reading Relecture Korrektur lesen:
Matthew Clarke, Marie-Pierre Santamarina, Anja Llorella

Art director Direction artistique Art Direktor:
Mireia Casanovas Soley

Graphic design and layout Mise en page et maquette Graphische Gestaltung und Layout:
Diego González

Printed by Imprimé par Gedruckt durch:
Anman Gràfiques del Vallès, Spain

ISBN: 3-8228-4172-2

Contents
Index
Inhalt

Introduction
Introduction
Einleitung

Once a social meeting place and public institution, nowadays the bathroom is for many a private oasis and refuge. The bathroom grew out of its purely functional role long ago and now enjoys the status of a room that harmoniously combines beauty and purpose.

The history and tradition of the bathroom are closely linked to basic human needs and are continually evolving since aspects of personal hygiene and well-being play an increasingly important role in our lives.

In ancient Greece, the bathroom was a place to come together and harmonize body and spirit. The Romans, however, considered the hygienic aspect more of a pleasant accompaniment to luxurious convivial pleasure.

As a result of changing bathing habits, public bathing facilities have been replaced by private baths over the centuries.

The first bathrooms were extremely large rooms, in which the toilet and dressing table were separated from the actual bathing area. Only towards the end of the 19th century did the bathroom become a place in which all hygiene-related elements were unified in one room.

Today, new materials and models, featuring original shapes, ensure that the bathroom serves the needs of both physical hygiene and relaxation even in a restricted space. So, by adhering to a series of formal guidelines, a small bathroom can thoroughly satisfy the needs of even the most demanding users. A well-thought out layout and the installation of custom-made furniture are basic requirements for the optimal use of existing floor space, and often the most creative designs are spurred by such constraints on space.

The selection of pale color schemes and light materials enhances the feeling of spaciousness while the use of glass and new, transparent materials helps to provide sufficient light in a bathroom. In addition, surface finishings are becoming more and more resistant to moisture and consequently more functional and easier to use.

Nowadays, the growing desire to create an attractive space that exudes well-being has resulted in a host of new and unique bathroom concepts, such as those presented in this book. The solutions provided range from purist to exotic/extravagant designs, often with an unmistakable influence of other cultures. The minimalist elements of the Japanese bathroom, for example, are the precursor of many current bathroom concepts.

Philippe Starck and Gianni Versace are only two examples of well-known designers who have applied themselves to bathroom design working with creators of fixtures and sanitary accessories such as Hoesch und Keramag. In *Small Bathrooms*, the works of these and other prominent designers and architects are presented, offering an overview of the latest trends and providing inspiration for modern and contemporary bathroom design.

Jadis, lieu de rencontre de la société et institution officielle, la salle de bains est devenue aujourd'hui une oasis privée, un refuge. Cela fait des lustres que la salle de bains est sortie des rangs de la pure fonctionnalité pour bénéficier désormais du statut de pièce représentative, où esthétique et fonction s'harmonisent à merveille.

L'histoire et la tradition de la salle de bains, étroitement liées aux besoins vitaux de l'homme, sont en constante évolution depuis l'importance prise par les soins corporels et le bien-être.

Dans la Grèce antique, le bain était un lieu de rencontre et servait à l'harmonie du corps et de l'esprit. Les Romains, quant à eux, mettaient plutôt l'accent sur l'aspect de l'hygiène que sur les bienfaits du bain pris en bonne compagnie, dans un cadre luxueux.

Au fil des siècles, suite aux modifications des habitudes liées au bain, les établissements de bains publics ont été remplacés par des bains privés.

Les premières salles de bains étaient des pièces surdimensionnées, dotées d'espaces séparés pour les toilettes et les coiffeuses. Il faudra attendre la fin du XIXe siècle pour voir l'apparition de la salle de bains comme un lieu réunissant en un seul espace tous les éléments liés à l'hygiène.

Aujourd'hui, de nouveaux modèles et matériaux innovants, associés à des formes originales, permettent à la salle de bains, même dans le cadre d'un espace réduit, de conjuguer hygiène corporelle et détente. La petite salle de bains, conditionnée par une série d'aspects formels, peut elle aussi satisfaire aux exigences de son utilisateur. Une distribution bien étudiée et l'intégration de meubles faits sur mesure sont les critères de base pour une utilisation optimale de la surface disponible. De cette réduction spatiale naissent souvent les designs les plus créatifs!

Le choix de tons clairs et de matériaux légers exalte la sensation d'espace. L'emploi du verre et de nouvelles matières transparentes permettent un bon éclairage de la salle de bains. En outre, le revêtement des surfaces offre une imperméabilité accrue à l'humidité garantissant ainsi un usage fonctionnel et un entretien facile.

Le besoin grandissant de voir la salle de bains se transformer en un lieu d'esthétique et de bien-être optimalisés, conduit à des concepts de salles de bains, novateurs et originaux, à l'instar de ceux qui sont présentés dans cet ouvrage. Les solutions proposées vont des concepts les plus puristes aux plus extravagants et même exotiques, où on ne saurait nier l'influence d'autres cultures. La salle de bains japonaise, par exemple, forte de son agencement minimaliste, est pionnière dans maints concepts de salles de bains actuelles.

Philippe Starck et Gianni Versace, pour ne citer que ces deux exemples de designers mondialement connus, se sont consacrés à la conception de salles de bains, en collaboration avec les producteurs de robinetteries et d'accessoires sanitaires, à l'instar de Hoesch et Keramag. Le livre, *Petites salles de bains*, présente les œuvres de ces designers et architectes de renom et d'autres encore, offrant un aperçu des nouvelles tendances, idées et inspirations pour une conception moderne et contemporaine de la salle de bains.

Einst gesellschaftlicher Treffpunkt und öffentliche Institution, stellt das Badezimmer heutzutage für viele eine private Oase und Zufluchtsort dar. Längst ist das Badezimmer über die reine Funktionalität herausgewachsen und genießt vielmehr den Status eines repräsentativen Raumes, der Ästhetik und Zweck harmonisch miteinander vereint.

Die Geschichte und Tradition des Badezimmers geht mit den Grundbedürfnissen des Menschen einher und entwickelt sich kontinuierlich weiter, seit Aspekte der Körperpflege und des Wohlbefindens für uns eine Rolle spielen.

Im antiken Griechenland war das Bad ein Ort des Zusammentreffens und diente der Harmonie zwischen Körper und Geist. Die Römer hingegen betrachteten den hygienischen Aspekt eher als einen angenehmen Begleiter des geselligen Vergnügens in luxuriösem Ausmaß.

Im Zuge der sich verändernden Badegewohnheiten wurden im Laufe der Jahrhunderte öffentliche Badeanstalten durch private Bäder ersetzt.

Die ersten Badezimmer waren groß dimensionierte Räume, von denen Toilette und Frisiertisch vom eigentlichen Badebereich getrennt waren, und erst gegen Ende des 19. Jahrhunderts entstand das Bad als ein Ort, in dem alle der Hygiene dienenden Elemente in einem Zimmer vereint wurden.

Heute sorgen neue Modelle und Materialen, sowie ausgefallene Formen selbst unter begrenzten räumlichen Bedingungen dafür, dass das Bad sowohl der Körperhygiene als auch der Entspannung dient. So kann das kleine Bad unter Beachtung einer Reihe formaler Aspekte durchaus den hohen Ansprüchen seiner Benutzer gerecht werden. Eine durchdachte Aufteilung und der Einbau maßgefertigter Möbel sind dabei die Grundvorrausetzungen für eine optimale Ausnutzung der vorhandenen Fläche und oftmals entsteht - gerade durch die Begrenzung des zur Verfügung stehenden Raumes - das kreativste Design.

Die Auswahl heller Farbtöne und leichter Materialien verstärkt darüber hinaus das Raumgefühl während durch die Verwendung von Glas und neuen, transparenten Werkstoffen für genügend Helligkeit gesorgt wird. Außerdem werden die Oberflächenverkleidungen immer widerstandsfähiger gegen Feuchtigkeit und garantieren somit einen funktionellen und pflegeleichten Gebrauch.

Der gestiegene Wunsch nach dem Bad als einem Ort des Wohlbefindens und maximaler Ästhetik bringt heutzutage eine Vielzahl von neuen und ausgefallenen Badkonzepten hervor, die in diesem Buch vorgestellt werden. Die dargestellten Lösungen reichen von puristischen bis hin zu exotisch-extravaganten Entwürfen und oftmals ist der Einfluss anderer Kulturen unverkennbar. Das japanische Bad beispielsweise, mit seinen auf ein Minimum reduzierten Elementen, ist der Vorreiter vieler aktueller Badkonzepte.

Philippe Starck und Gianni Versace sind nur zwei Beispiele weltberühmter Designer, die sich in Zusammenarbeit mit Herstellern von Armaturen und Sanitärzubehör wie Hoesch und Keramag der Badgestaltung gewidmet haben. In *Kleine Badezimmer* werden die Arbeiten dieser und weiterer namhafter Designer und Architekten vorgestellt, die einen Überblick der neusten Trends bieten und Anregung und Inspiration für eine moderne und zeitgemäße Badgestaltung liefern.

Design Aspects
Critères de design
Designaspekte

Various formal principles should be taken into consideration in the design and configuration of bathrooms. In small rooms, form and function should be tailored to the structure and technical conditions. The concepts which come out of these restricted requirements often produce a captivating originality and precision. Thus, for example, the selection of light materials and simple lines, as well as the well-structured configuration of space, can make a room appear larger. Good bathroom lighting also compensates for problems of space and can create stunning effects when combined with reflective materials and pale colors.

Divers critères doivent être pris en compte lors de la conception et de l'agencement d'une salle de bains. Dans les petits espaces, forme et fonction s'adapteront aux données structurelles et techniques. D'ailleurs, ces conditions limitées engendrent souvent des concepts qui séduisent par leur originalité et précision. Le choix de matériaux légers, par exemple, permet d'agrandir visuellement des lignes simples ou une distribution de l'espace bien structurée. En outre, un éclairage judicieux de la salle de bains masquera les problèmes de place : combiné à des matériaux réfléchissants et des couleurs claires, il peut créer des effets stupéfiants.

Es gibt unterschiedliche, formale Gesichtspunkte, die bei dem Entwurf und der Gestaltung von Badezimmern berücksichtigt werden sollten. Bei kleinen Räumen müssen Form und Funktion an die Struktur und die technischen Gegebenheiten angepasst werden. Die Konzepte, die unter diesen eingeschränkten Voraussetzungen entstehen, bestechen oftmals durch ihre Originalität und Präzision. So kann beispielsweise die Auswahl von leichten Materialien, eine einfache Linienführung sowie eine gut strukturierte Aufteilung den Raum optisch vergrößern. Eine gute Ausleuchtung des Badezimmers kaschiert zudem Platzprobleme und kann im Zusammenspiel mit reflektierenden Materialien und hellen Tönen verblüffende Effekte erzeugen.

Distribution	**Lighting**	**Materials**	**Colors**	**Capturing Space**
Distribution	Eclairage	Matériaux	Couleurs	Gain d'espace
Badaufteilung	Beleuchtung	Materialien	Farben	Platz gewinnen

Distribution Distribution Badaufteilung

The configuration of a bathroom requires intense planning, as changes in layout are particularly difficult after the installation of pipes and drainage spouts. The space available and the preferences of each individual user are critical in deciding whether or not a shower or bath should be chosen, if the bathroom should be open or closed and how much storage space is required.

La distribution de la salle de bains nécessite une excellente planification, car, après installation des conduites et des tuyaux d'évacuation d'eau, il est difficile de la modifier. La place disponible et les volontés de l'utilisateur sont des facteurs de décision essentiels, à savoir, installer une douche ou une baignoire, créer une salle de bains ouverte ou fermée et prévoir l'espace nécessaire au rangement.

Die Aufteilung des Badezimmers erfordert eine intensive Planung, weil nach Installierung der Leitungen und Abflussrohre eine Neuaufteilung äußerst schwierig wird. Der verfügbare Platz und die Wünsche jedes einzelnen Benutzers sind entscheidene Faktoren für die Entscheidung, ob eine Dusche oder eine Badewanne eingebaut wird, ob das Bad offen oder geschlossen ist und wieviel Stauraum benötigt wird.

Lighting Eclairage Beleuchtung

The ideal solution for a bathroom is the combination of adequate natural and artificial light. Natural light should be used as much as possible since it simplifies tasks such as shaving or putting on make-up. When using artificial light, it should be evenly spread. Light sources can be mounted from the ceiling or on the mirror or in furniture.

L'idéal pour une salle de bains est de parvenir à bien conjuguer lumière naturelle et artificielle. Lorsqu'il y a suffisamment de lumière naturelle, il faut en profiter au maximum, car elle facilite, entre autres, le rasage et le maquillage. Quant à la lumière artificielle, il faut veiller à une répartition harmonieuse de l'éclairage. Les sources de lumière peuvent être installées au plafond, autour du miroir ou sur les meubles.

Optimal für ein Badezimmer ist die Kombination aus ausreichend natürlichem und künstlichem Licht. Soweit natürliches Licht vorhanden ist, sollte in jedem Fall davon profitiert werden, denn natürliches Licht erleichtert Tätigkeiten wie Rasieren oder Schminken. Bei der Verwendung von künstlichem Licht sollte man auf eine gleichmäßige Ausleuchtung achten. Diese Lichtquellen können sowohl von der Decke herab, als auch am Spiegel oder in Möbeln montiert werden.

© Núria Fuentes

Materials Matériaux Materialien

The materials used in the bathroom should not only be decorative and easy to look after, but they should also be water-resistant. Classic materials such as tiles, wood and marble are now complemented by materials such as metal, cement, glass or stone, allowing a designer to explore various styles or develop new concepts.

Les matériaux employés dans la salle de bains doivent correspondre à certains critères, à savoir : beauté, entretien facile et résistance à l'eau. Les matériaux classiques, à savoir céramique, bois et marbre, sont aujourd'hui, souvent conjugués à d'autres matières comme le métal, le ciment, le verre ou la pierre, permettant au designer d'exalter différents styles ou, encore, de développer de nouveaux concepts.

Die verwendeten Materialien im Badezimmer sollten nicht nur dekorativ und pflegeleicht sein, sondern zudem auch wasserresistent. Die klassischen Materialien wie Keramik, Holz und Marmor werden heutzutage durch Werkstoffe wie Metall, Zement, Glas oder Stein ergänzt und erlauben es den Designern unterschiedliche Stilrichtungen zu betonen oder auch neue Konzepte zu entwickeln.

Stainless Steel Acier inoxydable Edelstahl

© Grey Crawford/Red Cover

Clay Argile Ton

© Jordi Sarrà

© Adriano Brusaforri

Wood Bois Holz

© Reto Guntli/Zapaimages

Marmor Marbre Marmor

© Flaminia

© Georges Fessy

Colors Couleurs Farben

The choice of colors should be based upon the taste of the user. In general, this means that pale, bright colors make the room seem larger and are therefore well suited to small bathrooms. Intense colors and combinations with rich contrasts can, however, be found in small bathrooms, giving them a distinctive atmosphere.

Certes, le choix des couleurs se fait en fonction du goût de l'utilisateur. Néanmoins, il faut savoir qu'en général les couleurs claires et lumineuses, donnant l'illusion d'agrandir la pièce, sont donc idéales pour les petites salles de bains. Ceci étant, ces espaces limités affichent parfois des tons intensifs et des combinaisons de couleurs très contrastées qui leur confèrent une ambiance unique.

Die Wahl der Farben sollte sich ganz nach dem Geschmack des Benutzers richten. Dabei gilt generell, dass helle und leuchtende Farben den Raum optisch größer wirken lassen und deshalb für kleine Badezimmer besonders geeignet sind. Dennoch findet man auch in kleinen Bädern intensive Töne und kontrastreiche Farbkombinationen, die diesen Räumen ein unverwechselbares Ambiente verleihen können.

Green Vert Grün

© Jordi Sarrà

Yellow Jaune Gelb

Red Rouge Rot

© Jordi Miralles

Blue Bleu Blau

Violet Violet Violett

Capturing Space Gain d'espace Platz gewinnen

This chapter presents various ways of making small rooms appear larger. For example, the use of translucent materials such as glass and acrylic visually enlarges a space. The same is true of pale, bright colors, along with mirrors and reflective surfaces. Finally, taking full advantage of available light sources can make a room appear substantially larger.

Ce chapitre présente mille et une possibilités d'élargissement optique de petits espaces. L'emploi de matériaux translucides, à l'instar du verre et de l'acrylique, permet d'agrandir visuellement l'espace. On obtient le même effet, en utilisant des couleurs claires et lumineuses ou en installant des miroirs ou des surfaces réfléchissantes. Enfin, l'optimalisation de toutes les sources de lumière existantes permet d'obtenir aussi une étonnante sensation d'amplitude spatiale.

In diesem Kapitel werden die unterschiedlichsten Möglichkeiten vorgestellt, um kleine Räume optisch zu vergrößern. So führt die Verwendung von lichtdurchlässigen Materialien wie Glas oder Acryl zu einer Erweiterung des Raumeindrucks. Ebenso verhält es sich mit dem Gebrauch heller und leuchtender Farben sowie der Anbringung von Spiegeln und verspiegelten Oberflächen im Allgemeinen. Schließlich erzielt man einen erheblichen Vergrößerungseffekt durch die maximale Ausschöpfung der vorhandenen Lichtquellen.

© Jan Verlinde, Ludo Noël

Styles and Types
Styles et modèles
Stile und Typen

Nowadays, it is not always easy to assign clearly defined styles to bathrooms, since more and more designers are using a mixture of various elements. A dominant style, however, can usually be recognized; it is usually combined with diverse decorative elements. The style can be determined either by the design of the bathroom installation or the layout. So the minimalist style, for example, is characterized by soft colors and light materials, supplemented by clean lines and forms. The layout of a bathroom decides whether it is a bathroom with a view, a compact bathroom or an open bathroom.

De nos jours, il n'est pas toujours évident de définir le style précis des salles de bains. En effet, de plus en plus de designers mélangent les éléments de styles différents. Malgré cela, un style domine toujours, ponctué de divers éléments de décoration et définissable par le design de l'installation même ou par la distribution des pièces. Le style minimaliste, par exemple, est reconnaissable par la douceur des tons et la légèreté des matériaux, auxquelles s'ajoute la pureté des lignes et des formes. En fonction de l'agencement spatial des salles de bains, il est possible d'en différencier plusieurs types : salle de bains avec vue, compact e ou ouverte.

Heutzutage ist es nicht immer einfach, Badezimmer eindeutig definierten Stilrichtungen zuzuordnen, da zunehmend mehr Designer eine Mischung verschiedener Stilelemente verwenden. Ein dominierender Stil ist dennoch meist zu erkennen, in der Regel kombiniert mit diversen Dekorationselementen. Die Stilrichtung kann sowohl durch das Design der Badeinrichtung, als auch durch die Raumaufteilung bestimmt werden. So ist der minimalistische Stil beispielsweise durch sanfte Töne und leichte Materialien geprägt, die durch klare Linien und Formen ergänzt werden. Die räumliche Anordnung der Bäder entscheidet darüber, ob es sich um ein Badezimmer mit Aussicht, ein kompaktes oder ein offenes Badezimmer handelt.

With a View
Avec vue
Mit Aussicht

Avantgarde
Avant-gardiste
Avantgardistisch

Contemporary
Contemporain
Zeitgenössisch

Minimalist
Minimaliste
Minimalistisch

Maximalist
Maximaliste
Maximalistisch

Romantic
Romantique
Romantisch

Rustic
Rustique
Rustikal

Exotic
Exotique
Exotisch

Open
Ouvert
Offen

Compact
Compact
Kompakt

With a View Avec vue Mit Aussicht

In this chapter, attractive views are shown, as a large window over the bathtub or glass doors, which look out on to the surrounding landscape. The priority here is to be able to see from inside to outside without being open to view in the opposite direction.

Que ce soit une grande fenêtre au-dessus de la baignoire ou des portes en verre laissant transparaître la vue sur le paysage environnant, ce chapitre présente des salles de bains dont la spécificité est de bénéficier d'une belle vue de l'intérieur vers l'extérieur et non dans le sens inverse.

Sei es ein großes Fenster über der Badewanne oder Glastüren, die den Blick auf die umgebende Landschaft gestatten - in diesem Kapitel werden Badezimmer vorgestellt, die sich alle durch eine reizvolle Aussicht auszeichnen. Dabei gilt es zu beachten, dass die Sicht von innen nach außen, nicht aber in umgekehrter Richtung ermöglicht wird.

© Montse Garriga

Avantgarde Avant-gardiste Avantgardistisch

In this chapter, projects with a modern, contemporary design are shown. Metal and glass as well as synthetic coatings in intense colors are the most commonly used materials. These artistically shaped bathtubs and sinks are not only attractive, but also comfortable and practical.

Ce chapitre réunit des projets caractérisés par un design moderne, contemporain Les matériaux employés pour ce genre de salles de bains sont souvent le métal, le verre, les matières synthétiques aux couleurs intenses. Les baignoires et lavabos aux formes artistiques ne sont pas seulement beaux, ils offrent aussi confort et commodité.

In diesem Kapitel werden Projekte zusammengefasst, die alle durch ein modernes, zeitgenössisches Design geprägt sind. Häufig verwendete Materialien sind bei diesen Bädern Metall und Glas sowie Kunststoffbeschichtungen in intensiven Farben. Die kunstvoll geschnittenen Badewannen und Waschbecken sind in der Regel nicht nur attraktiv, sondern auch bequem und praktisch.

Contemporary Contemporain Zeitgenössisch

Contemporary bathrooms are classified geometrically and practically in the following three areas: vanity, wet area and toilet area. Building materials such as marble, wood and synthetics are used in well-balanced colors to ensure timeless, elegant design.

En général, les salles de bains contemporaines affichent une organisation spatiale géométrique et pratique des trois zones suivantes : plan de toilette, zone humide et toilettes. Les matériaux comme le marbre, le bois et les matières synthétiques, se déclinent dans des coloris équilibrés pour créer un design intemporel et élégant.

Zeitgenössische Badezimmer zeichnen sich vor allem durch eine geometrische und praktische Unterteilung in folgende drei Hauptbereiche aus: Waschtisch, Nassbereich und Toilettenbereich. Werkstoffe wie Marmor, Holz und Kunststoff werden in ausgewogenen Farbtönen verwendet und sorgen für ein zeitloses und elegantes Design.

Minimalist Minimaliste Minimalistisch

In the bathrooms included in this style category, there is a minimum of furniture and maximum of light. An Asian influence is often discernible in these bathroom concepts. The preference is for black and white, with only a few elements set in an open layout. This is intended to transmit a feeling of peace and relaxation.

Les salles de bains qui répondent à cette tendance stylistique conjuguent un minimum de mobilier et un maximum de lumière. On y ressent de toute évidence l'influence asiatique, avec une préférence pour les salles de bains noir et blanc, déclinant un minimum d'éléments, dans un espace ouvert propice au repos et à la détente.

Bei den unter dieser Stilrichtung zusammengefassten Bädern, trifft ein Minimum an Mobiliar auf ein Maximum an Licht. Oft ist bei diesen Badkonzepten der asiatische Einfluss unverkennbar. Hier werden vorzugsweise weiße und dunkle Bäder, mit wenigen Elementen in einer offenen Anordnung entworfen. Dadurch soll das Gefühl von Ruhe und Entspannung vermittelt werden.

© Falper

© Falper

© Núria Fuentes

Maximalist Maximaliste Maximalistisch

Luxurious, ostentatious purple decorations as well as explosive colors characterize this style. Maximalism refers to the aesthetic of the 18th and 19th centuries, combined with elements from the 50s, 60s and 70s. These are extravagant bathrooms that reflect the personality of the user in a special way.

Décorations exubérantes, fioritures pourprées, pompeuses et couleurs explosives définissent ce style. Le maximalisme s'oriente sur l'esthétique des XVIIIe et XIXe siècles en la combinant à des éléments des années cinquante, soixante et soixante-dix. Cela donne des salles de bains extravagantes qui reflètent de façon particulière la personnalité de leur utilisateur.

Üppige, prunkvolle Purpurdekorationen sowie explosive Farben kennzeichnen diesen Stil. Der Maximalismus orientiert sich dabei an der Ästhetik des 18. und 19. Jahrhunderts und kombiniert diese mit Elementen der 50er, 60er und 70er Jahre. So entstehen extravagante Bäder, die in besonderer Art und Weise die Persönlichkeit ihrer Benutzer reflektieren.

Sentiment and fantasy are the key words of 18th-century Romanticism. This is mirrored in the love of details and baroque decorative elements. For Romantic baths, traditional materials such as stone, wood and marble are most commonly used, usually in pastel colors.

Sentiments et fantaisie, mots clés du romantisme du XVIIIe siècle, se reflètent dans ce style par un amour des détails et une décoration tout en fioritures. Les salles de bains romantiques emploient souvent des matériaux classiques, à l'instar de la pierre, du bois et du marbre qui se déclinent principalement dans une gamme de tons pastel.

Gefühl und Fantasie sind die Schlüsselwörter der Romantik des 18. Jahrhunderts und spiegeln sich bei diesem Stil in großer Detailliebe und verschnörkelten Dekorationselementen wider. Bei romantischen Bädern sind klassische Werkstoffe wie Stein, Holz und Marmor die am häufigsten verwendeten Materialien. Sie werden überwiegend in sanften Pastelltönen gehalten.

The projects shown in this chapter are the expression of a lifestyle that reflects direct contact with nature. The primary feature here is the use of stark, natural materials with few ornaments. Tiles are made of terra cotta or burnished sandstone, natural stone or cement. These materials are often combined with dark wood.

Les projets présentés dans ce chapitre sont l'expression d'un style de vie qui reflète le contact direct avec la nature. Sa caractéristique principale est l'emploi de matériaux naturels, sobres et dépourvus de fioritures. Les préférences vont vers le carrelage en terre cuite ou en grés flammé, pierre naturelle ou ciment. Ces matières se conjuguent souvent au bois foncé.

Die in diesem Kapitel vorgestellten Projekte gelten als Ausdruck eines Lebensstils, der den direkten Kontakt mit der Natur widerspiegelt. Hauptmerkmal ist hier die Verwendung natürlicher und schlichter Materialien mit wenigen Verzierungen. Besonders beliebt sind Fliesen aus Terrakotta oder gebranntem Ton, Naturstein oder Zement. Kombiniert werden diese Werkstoffe oftmals mit dunklem Holz.

Exotic Exotique Exotisch

The exotic style is inspired by the esthetics of tropical, Caribbean and African cultures. The materials required by the climate of these regions due to climate, such as bamboo and natural stone, are prepared and combined with durable, high-grade synthetic materials. Bright colors and hand-finished decorative elements emphasize this style and add a finishing touch.

Le design de style exotique s'inspire de l'esthétique de zones tropicales. Les matériaux employés dans ces pays en fonction du climat, à l'instar du bambou et de la pierre naturelle, sont traités et combinés à des matières synthétiques résistantes, de qualité supérieure. Couleurs éclatantes et décoration artisanale exaltent ce style et lui confèrent la touche finale.

Das Design im exotischen Stil greift die Ästhetik tropischer, karibischer und afrikanischer Kulturen auf. Die dort aufgrund des Klimas verwendeten Materialien, wie Bambusholz und Naturstein, werden aufbereitet und mit widerstandsfähigen, hochwertigen Kunststoffen kombiniert. Leuchtende Farben und handgefertigte Dekorationselemente unterstreichen diesen Stil und geben ihm die entscheidende Note.

Open Ouvert Offen

Open bathrooms are particularly well suited to a house with only one occupant. The lack of doors and the use of transparent room dividers are the hallmarks of this bathroom concept. In this layout, the toilet should be out of sight while the decorative elements are in the forefront.

Le concept de salles de bains ouvertes convient particulièrement bien aux célibataires. L'absence de portes et l'emploi de cloisons transparentes en sont les caractéristiques essentielles. La planification d'une telle salle de bains doit prévoir de masquer les toilettes et de mettre les éléments de décoration au premier plan.

Offene Bäder eignen sich besonders für Single-Haushalte. Das Fehlen von Türen und die Verwendung transparenter Raumteiler sind die wesentlichen Merkmale dieses Badezimmerkonzeptes. Beachtet werden sollte bei dieser Planung, dass sich die Toilette ausserhalb der Sichtweite befindet, während die dekorativen Elemente in den Vordergrund rücken sollten.

© Virgina del Giudice

The bathrooms presented in this chapter are characterized by a compact layout and therefore offer optimal solutions for limited spaces. Horizontal lines are left as fluid as possible and as a result, the furniture and bathroom elements are usually arranged in a vertical configuration.

Les salles de bains présentées dans ce chapitre se définissent par une distribution spatiale compacte et offrent des solutions optimales qui se mesurent à l'aune des mètres carrés. Les lignes horizontales aussi fluides que possible définissent, la plupart du temps la verticalité de l'agencement des meubles et éléments de salle de bains.

Die in diesem Kapitel vorgestellten Bäder sind durch eine kompakte Raumaufteilung gekennzeichnet und bieten somit optimale Lösungsvorschläge für eine begrenzte Quadratmeterzahl. Horizontale Linien werden so weit wie möglich frei gelassen und entsprechend erscheint die Anordnung der Bademöbel und - elemente überwiegend in vertikaler Form.

Designers
Designers
Designer

Gianni Versace, Wolfgang Joop, Porsche Design Team and Philippe Starck are not names generally associated with bathrooms. Their usual creative fields are the fashion industry, the automobile industry and architecture. These renowned designers all have something in common: a strong sense for beauty as well as an extravagant and expressive stylistic signature. Because of this, renowned manufacturers of sanitary fixtures such as Keramag und Hoesch have requested designs for their collections in order to satisfy the growing needs of their clients.

Gianni Versace, Wolfgang Joop, Porsche Design Team et Philippe Starck sont des noms que l'on n'associe pas automatiquement aux salles de bains. Ils sont davantage liés au secteur de la mode, à l'industrie automobile ou à l'architecture, leurs ateliers de création habituels. Ces grands noms du design ont néanmoins un point commun : un sens aigu de l'esthétique accompagné d'une griffe à la fois extravagante et expressive. C'est la raison pour laquelle les grands fabricants d'installations sanitaires, à l'instar de Keramag et Hoesch, font appel à ces designers pour concevoir leurs collections, pour satisfaire les exigences toujours croissantes de leur clientèle.

Gianni Versace, Wolfgang Joop, Porsche Design Team und Philippe Starck sind Namen, die man nicht unbedingt mit Badezimmern in Verbindung bringt. Eher ordnet man sie der Modebranche, der Autoindustrie oder der Architektur zu, ihren eigentlichen Schöpferstuben. Dennoch weisen diese renommierten Designer eine Gemeinsamkeit auf: ein maximaler Sinn für Ästhetik sowie eine extravagante und expressive Designhandschrift. Aus diesem Grund haben renommierte Hersteller von Sanitätszubehör wie Keramag und Hoesch diese Designer für die Entwürfe ihrer Kollektionen beauftragt, um die ständig wachsenden Ansprüche ihrer Kunden zu befriedigen.

Versace

Joop

Porsche

Philippe Starck

© Tom Whipps

The Italian fashion designer Gianni Versace is known around the world for his flashy and eccentric designs with flamboyant colors, cuts and materials. Versace was also successful in other areas, such as interior design. He also designed a collection of dream bathrooms with Ceramiche Gardenia Orchidea.

Le créateur de mode italien, Gianni Versace, est connu dans le monde entier pour son design excentrique et extraordinaire aux couleurs, coupes et matières spectaculaires. Versace a eu également beaucoup de succès dans d'autres domaines, à savoir l'agencement d'intérieurs. Il a conçu, entre autres, une collection de salles de bains de rêve en collaboration avec Ceramiche Gardenia Orchidea.

Der italienische Modeschöpfer Gianni Versace ist auf der ganzen Welt für sein schrilles und außergewöhnliches Design mit auffallenden Farben, Schnitten und Materialien bekannt. Auch in anderen Bereichen, wie der Raumgestaltung, war Versace erfolgreich und entwarf unter anderem eine Kollektion von Traumbädern in Zusammenarbeit mit Ceramiche Gardenia Orchidea.

© Versace Ceramic Design

JOOP!

Under the name of the founder Wolfgang Joop who is now achieving global success with his new couture line Wunderkind, the Joop Living Team is working with renowned partners like Keramag and Koralle to develop a new bathroom series. The models range from the unconventional Lounge bathroom to a classic bathroom and a luxurious Boudoir bathroom.

Sous le nom du fondateur Wolfgang Joop, qui remporte actuellement un succès mondial avec sa ligne de couture Wunderkind, le Joop Living Team s'est associé à des partenaires renommés tels que Keramag et Koralle, pour développer une gamme de salles de bains. Les modèles vont de la salle de bains non-conventionnelle Lounge aux salles de bains de luxe Boudoir en passant par la salle de bains classique.

Unter dem Namen des Gründers Wolfgang Joop, der jetzt mit seiner neuen Couture Linie Wunderkind weltweite Erfolge erzielt, hat das Joop Living Team in Zusammenarbeit mit renommierten Partnern wie Keramag und Koralle eine Badserie entwickelt. Die Modelle reichen von einem unkonventionellen Lounge Bad über das klassische Pool Bad bis hin zum luxuriösen Boudoir Bad.

The name Porsche stands for class, elegance, style and comfort. Sports vehicles from the German manufacturer are sought after all over the world. Porsche Design has made its mark not only in the automobile industry but has also been commissioned by Keramag to design the F1 bathroom collection with natural lines and angular surfaces.

Le nom Porsche est l'image de marque alliant classique, élégance, style et confort. Les voitures de sport de la firme allemande sont admirées dans le monde entier. Mais le secteur automobile n'est pas le seul à porter haut les couleurs de l'illustre Porsche Design qui a également développé, à la demande de Keramag, la collection de salles de bains F1, avec ses lignes naturelles et ses surfaces coupées à l'oblique.

Der Name Porsche steht stellvertretend für Klassik, Eleganz, Stil und Komfort, und die Sportwagen aus dem deutschen Hause sind auf der ganzen Welt begehrt. Porsche Design seine ihre markante Note nicht nur im Automobilbereich gesetzt, sondern hat mit einer natürlichen Linienführung und schrägen Schnittebenen im Auftrag von Keramag auch die Badkollektion F1 entwickelt.

S+ARCK

Philippe Starck is considered the *enfant terrible* of the design world. His world-famous creations range from a toothbrush to a TV set to a hotel in New York. He has also been active in interior design and, together with the manufacturers Hoesch and Duravit, he designed a series of unique bathroom collections.

Philippe Starck est réputé pour être l'enfant terrible du monde du design. Les créations mondialement connues de cet architecte d'intérieur vont de la brosse à dents au téléviseur en passant par un hôtel à New York. Mais le Français s'est aussi fait un nom dans l'agencement d'intérieurs et il a conçu, en collaboration avec les fabricants Hoesch et Duravit, une série de collections de salles de bains extraordinaires.

Philippe Starck gilt als *enfant terrible* der Designer-Welt und die weltweit bekannten Kreationen des Innenarchitekten reichen von der Zahnbürste über den Fernseher bis zum New Yorker Hotel. Auch auf dem Gebiet der Raumgestaltung war der Franzose nicht untätig und er entwarf in Zusammenarbeit mit den Herstellern Hoesch und Duravit eine Reihe aussergewöhnlicher Badkollektionen.

© Hoesch

Fittings and Accessories
Equipement sanitaire et accessoires
Sanitäre Einrichtungen und Zubehörteile

The style of a bathroom is largely defined by the choice of sanitary accessories. Toilets, bidets, sinks and bathtubs or showers from the same collection are often combined, but models from different manufacturers can also be mixed together. In the case of small bathrooms, a shower saves space and so it is preferable to a bathtube. Accessories marry functionality with visual attractiveness, as evidenced in the latest toilet-paper holders, which are not only practical but also decorative and original.

Le choix de l'équipement sanitaire est essentiel dans la définition du style de la salle de bains. La plupart du temps, toilettes, bidet, lavabo et baignoire ou douche sont choisis dans la même gamme mais, de plus en plus, la tendance est de combiner les éléments de différentes marques entre eux. Dans les petites salles de bains, la douche représente un gain de place, et de ce fait, son installation est préférable à celle d'une baignoire. Les accessoires allient performance fonctionnelle et esthétique sublimée, à l'instar, par exemple, des supports de papier de toilette, fonctionnels, décoratifs et originaux.

Mit der Auswahl der sanitären Einrichtungen wird der Stil des Badezimmers weitgehend definiert. Häufig werden Toilette, Bidet, Waschbecken und Badewanne bzw. Dusche aus der selben Kollektion verwendet, oft aber auch Modelle unterschiedlicher Anbieter miteinander kombiniert. Bei kleinen Badezimmern ist der platzsparende Einbau einer Dusche dem einer Badewanne vorzuziehen. Die Zubehörteile verbinden eine äußerst praktische Funktion mit einer ausgefeilten Ästhetik. Dies zeigt sich am Beispiel neuer Toilettenpapierhalter, die zweckmäßig, dekorativ und orginell zugleich sind.

Bathtubs
Baignoires
Badewannen

Showers
Douches
Duschen

Sinks
Lavabos
Waschbecken

Toilets and Bidets
Toilettes et bidets
Toiletten und Bidets

Furniture
Meubles
Möbel

Fixtures and Accessories
Robinetterie et accessoires
Armaturen und Zubehör

Bathtubs Baignoires Badewannen

Acrylic or metaacrylate are the materials most often used to manufacture of bathtubs. These materials are water-resistant, durable and highly efficient in retaining heat. Furthermore, they allow for substancial variations in design.

L'acrylique ou méthacrylique sont des matériaux employés actuellement pour la fabrication de baignoires. Ces matières, à la fois imperméables et résistantes, ont une grande capacité de conservation de la chaleur. De surcroît, elles permettent de créer tout un éventail de designs variés.

Acryl oder Metaacrylat sind die Materialien, die heutzutage am häufigsten für die Herstellung von Badewannen verwendet werden. Diese Werkstoffe sind wasserressistent, widerstandsfähig und verfügen über eine hohe Kapazität, Temperaturen zu halten. Darüber hinaus erlauben sie große Variationsmöglichkeiten im Design.

Showers Douches Duschen

Showers are recommended in small bathrooms since they take up less space than a bathtub. The choice is varied and ranges from square to rectangular to corner installations. Free-standing showers are very popular in small bathrooms.

Dans les petites salles de bains, il est conseillé d'installer une douche qui prendra moins de place qu'une baignoire. L'offre des modèles est multiple et se décline au gré des formes carrées, rectangulaires ou angulaires. Les colonnes de douche sont aussi très appréciées dans les petits espaces, car ce sont des monoblocs indépendants.

In kleinen Bädern ist der Einbau einer Dusche empfehlenswert, da sie weniger Platz als eine Badewanne benötigt. Das Angebot ist vielfältig und reicht von quadratischen - über rechteckige - bis zu Über - Eck - Installationen. Sehr beliebt für kleine Räume sind auch Duschsäulen, die freistehend montiert werden.

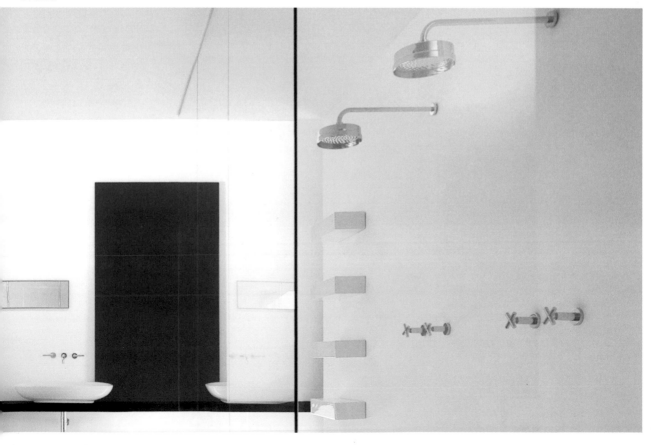

© Hoesch

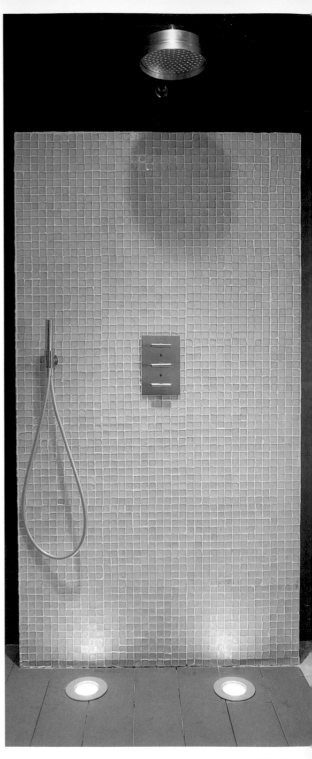

© Cesana

© Flaminia

Sinks Lavabos Waschbecken

The range of sinks on the market is varied and caters to various needs and space requirements: some can be mounted to a wall and be only 12in in diameter, while others can be fitted into furniture elements or set on stands.

L'éventail d'offre de lavabos est large et propose des solutions au gré des besoins et des espaces les plus divers : modèles muraux, d'un diamètre de 30 cm, fixés au mur, modèles intégrés dans le mobilier ou installés sur un socle.

Das Angebot an Waschbecken ist vielfältig und bietet Möglichkeiten für die unterschiedlichsten Bedürfnisse und räumlichen Gegebenheiten: Es gibt Modelle ,die an der Wand montiert werden und über einen Durchmesser von nur 30 cm verfügen; Modelle, die ins Mobiliar integriert sind oder auf Sockel gebaute Konstruktionen.

© Sanico

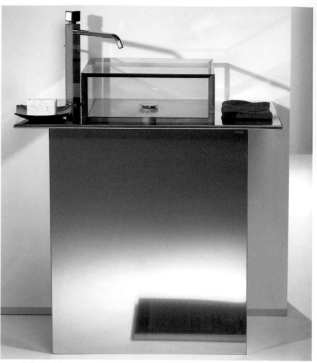

© Orpan Advance

© Orpan Advance

© Ritmonio

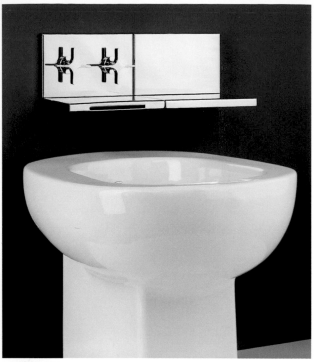

© Ritmonio

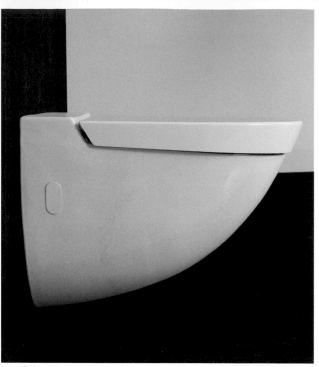

© Keramag

Furniture Meubles Möbel

Bathroom furniture must be, above all, water-resistant and moisture-resistant. The selection of furniture depends storage requirements. In small bathrooms, lower cabinet on rollers are especially suitable as they can easily be stored under a sink.

Le mobilier de salle de bains doit en première ligne être résistant à l'eau et à l'humidité. Le choix des meubles dépend des besoins en rangement. Pour les petites salles de bains, les armoires sur roulettes sont particulièrement bien indiquées, car elles sont faciles à installer sous le lavabo.

Das Mobiliar im Badezimmer muß in erster Linie wasser- und feuchtigkeitsresistent sein. Die Auswahl der Möbel hängt von dem benötigten Stauraumbedarf ab. Für kleine Bäder sind rollbare Unterschränke besonders geeignet, das sie bequem unter dem Waschbecken verstaut werden können.

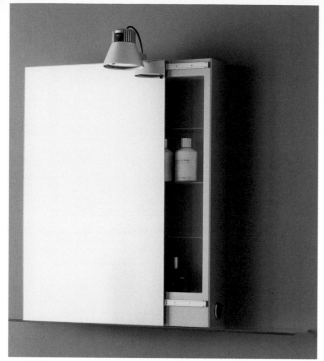

© Alape

© Permesso

© Alape

Fixtures and Accessories Robinetterie et accessoires Armaturen und Zubehör

Fixtures and accessories are significant components of the bathroom. Some of today's most creative designs are found in the comprehensive selection of faucets, soap dishes and toothbrush holders. They are important style elements and give the bathroom a distinctive, decorative feel.

La robinetterie et autres accessoires sont des éléments essentiels dans la salle de bains. L'offre abondante de robinets, porte-savons et supports à brosses à dents décline les designs les plus originaux. Eléments de style essentiels, ils confèrent à la salle de bains, la note décorative finale.

Armaturen und andere Zuebhörteile sind wesentliche Bestandteile des Bades. Bei dem reichhaltigen Angebot an Wasserhähnen, Seifenspendern und Zahnbürstenhaltern sind die ausgefallendsten Designs zu finden. Sie sind ein wichtiges Stilelement und geben dem Badezimmer die entscheidende, dekorative Note.

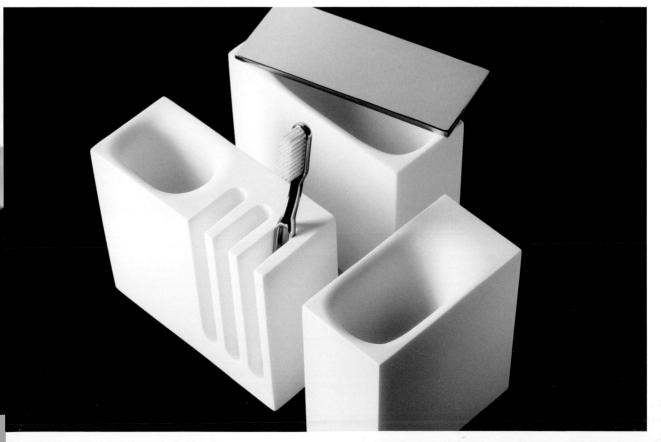

© Sanico

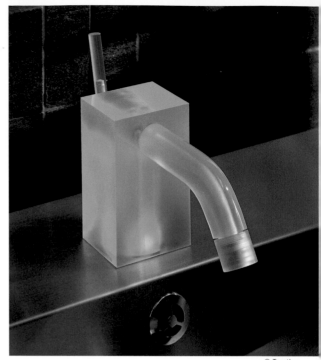

© Trentino

© Sanico

© Duilio Bitetto

© Sanico

Special thanks to Remerciements particuliers à Mit besonderem Dank an

A Prima
A-cero Arquitectos
AEM
Alan Faena
Alape
Alberto Kalach
Althea Ceramica
Ana Peña
Ana Simó
Archikubik
Augusto Le Monnier, Lorna Agustí, Natalia G. Novelles
Brooks Graham
Cecconi Simone
Ceramiche Gardenia Orchidea
Charlie Barnett Associates
Claudio Silvestrin Architects
Dornbracht
Dorotea Olivia
Dry Diseño
Duggie Fields
Duravit
E. Navazo, L. G. Guzmán, R. Alonso Yáñez
Esperanza García Aubert
Eva Dallo
Falper
Flaminia
Héctor Restrepo Calvo/Heres Arquitectura
Hoesch
Holger Kleine
Inés Lobo
Janson Goldstein
Jennifer Randall & Associates
Jo Crepain Architects
John Cockings Architects
Kalhöfer-Korschildgen

Keramag
Kim/Starck Network
Lizarriturry Tuneu Arquitectures
Luis Benedit
Marianne Fassler
Michael Carapetian
Michael Davis
Minim Arquitectos
Nancy Robbins, Lluís Victori
Navarro/Zalaja
Nil Solà
Nina Hallwachs/Porsche Design Group
Nora Rochlitzer/Wunderkind
Original Vision
Orpan Advance
Pablo Chiaporri
Patrick Schleifer
Permesso
Petrovic & Partner
Propeller Z
Putu Suarsa
Renato D'Ettorre
Ritmonio
Sanico
Shigeru Ban
Sieger Design
Silvia Rademakers, Virginia Palleres
Simon Vélez
Stefania Spallanzani/Foletti & Petrillo Design
Stéphan Bourgeois
Stephen Varady Architecture
Ann Sacks/Tate & Kuo Lavatories
Teresa Sepulcre
Trentino
Virginia Bates